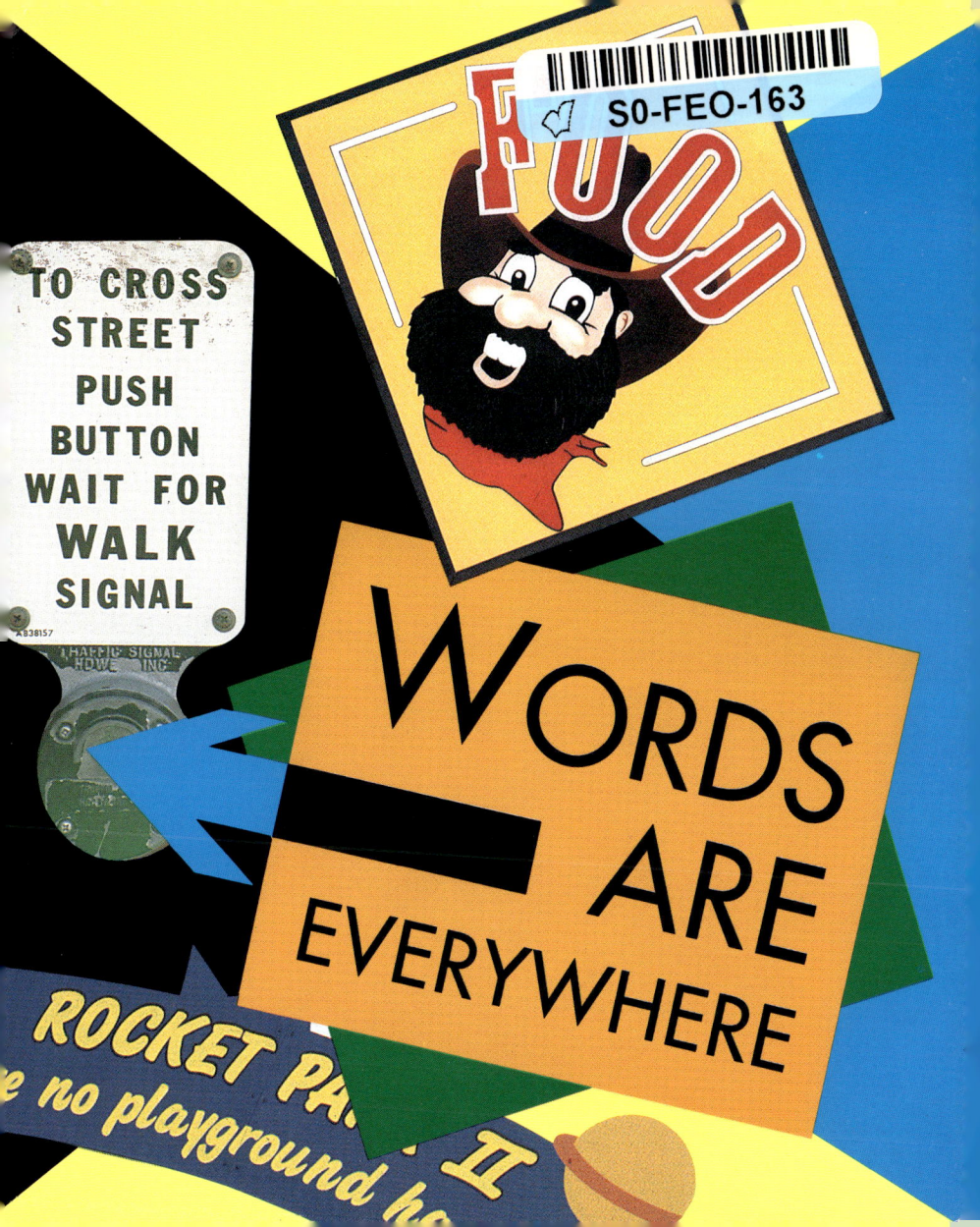

Words Are Everywhere

Words are everywhere.

Words help
to keep us safe.

TO CROSS STREET PUSH BUTTON WAIT FOR WALK SIGNAL

SLIPPERY ROCKS

CAUTION

ELDERLY PEOPLE CROSS HERE

BUCKLE UP IT'S THE LAW

Words tell us
where we can get help.

POLICE
HOSPITAL
POLICE
AA
AUCKLAND
ACCIDENT & EMERGENCY
CLINIC OPEN 7 DAYS

Words help us
to find our way.

Nature Trails

←

Visitor Information 100m

9

Words tell us
what we cannot do.

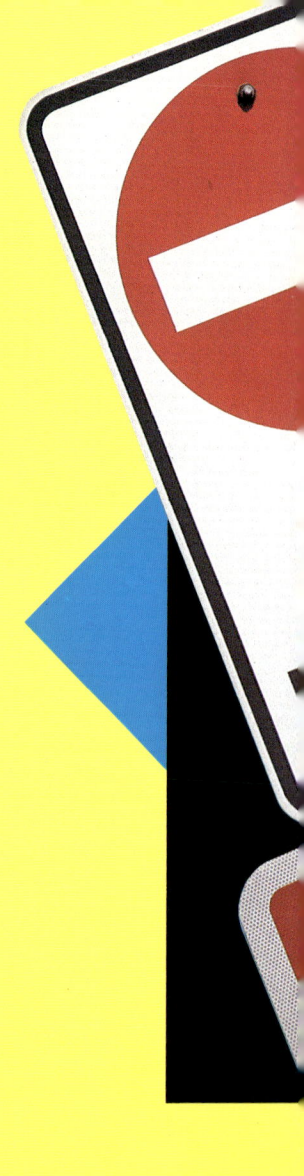

11

Words tell us what things are.

13

Words help
to protect our earth.

'DO THE RIGHT THING'
DON'T LITTER
PHS
nly
NOW
AREA OF
RE RISK
NG OF FIRES
OHIBITED
Caution
Caterpillars
At Work

Words are everywhere.